CAMPER VANS
AND RVs
IN PICTURES

Contents

4

38

18

28

CAMPER VANs AND RVs

Preface	4
Development of the Camper Van	8
Travelling by Camper Van	18
The Campsite Experience	24
Everyday Life	28
The Hippie Lifestyle	34
The Camper Van on Screen	38
Customisation and Conversions	48
Afterword	60

48

First published in the UK in 2011 by Instinctive Product Development

© Instinctive Product Development 2012

www.instinctivepd.com

Printed in China

ISBN: 978-1-907657-74-0

Designed by: BrainWave

Creative Director: Kevin Gardner

Written by: Henry Hirst

Images courtesy of Shutterstock, Magic Car Pics, Creative Commons and Richard Evans

Preface

Of all the revolutions that affected the history of the 20th century, the revolution in transport represented by the development of the internal combustion engine at the end of the 19th century was perhaps the most profound. Once produced in massive numbers, the cost of the petrol and diesel engine declined rapidly, making motoring accessible to an ever-greater proportion of the population. Countless millions, spurred on by the development of the mass-market car, such as the Model T Ford, discovered the attraction of the open road and, as traffic increased, so the road network improved with the development of trunk roads from the 1930s onwards.

Alongside the development of the internal combustion engine, there were also other changes in society that altered the perception of the road vehicle. As society, particularly in Europe and North America, became more prosperous, so individuals and families had more leisure time; with improving living standards and, for the first time, the ability to take more regular and longer holidays, the traditional week at a seaside resort was no longer a given. Increased prosperity and better health provision also led to a gradual increase in the life expectancy of the general population and, with this, the possibility of a longer and healthier retirement. Thus it was that the camper van, in its various guises and sizes, developed.

■ **BELOW:** A 'recreational vehicle' or RV parked up at camp.

Whilst, to many, the classic Volkswagen model dating originally from the 1950s epitomises the typical camper van, in reality there was and remains a great variety of such vehicles in size and in the range of equipment fitted. At one extreme there is the massive Winnebago-type vehicle; these are, perhaps, better described as motor homes given the quality and range of the internal fittings and would not, perhaps, be regarded by true aficionados as 'real' camper vans given that the camper van was originally designed to be cheap to purchase and operate. These motor homes are often fitted with showers, toilets and have the facility for transporting a smaller secondary vehicle; facilities

■ **ABOVE:** Mercedes and VW transporters.

that the more basic camper van lacks. These vehicles are known widely, particularly in the USA, as Recreational Vehicles (RVs).

There are a number of 'traditional' style camper vans that have existed alongside the familiar Volkswagen. Many of these are conversions from other proprietary models of van. Examples include the 'Overcab'. These vehicles are again bigger than the conventional VW-type of camper van, and feature an extension of the purpose-built body over the top of the existing van cab. This space is often used to provide accommodation for a bed. Overcab vans have been converted from a number of models, including the Ford Transit and the Renault Master. Other vehicle types with fixed roofs include the 'High Top', which is simply a conversion of an existing high-bodied van;

■ **BELOW:** A Type 2 VW camper van visiting a windmill!

■ **ABOVE & BELOW:** The launch of the Bedford Dormobile.

an example of this would be the Autosleeper Harmony. The 'Low Profile' also has a specialist body but without the overcab extension. One means of increasing the headroom was to have a roof capable of being raised whilst the vehicle was stationary. Here the main section of the roof can be raised with protection from the elements being provided by canvas sides and ends. 'Raised Roof' models included conversions of the classic Volkswagen models and the Ford Transit. The final significant variant, and perhaps the successor to the 'classic' camper van, was the 'Fixed Roof' model. These vehicles, that included the Mercedes-Benz Vito and the Volkswagen Transporter, are relatively small with more basic facilities.

In Britain, the name 'Dormobile' was often used as a generic term for the camper van; this derived from the launch in 1957 of the conversion of the Bedford CA van. The Dormobile, converted at a factory in Folkestone, was the result of a change to the British tax laws; previous conversions had been classed by the tax authorities as an estate car and thus incurred Purchase Tax. Provided that the new conversion included equipment deemed to be capable of supporting life – such as a cooker – Purchase Tax was not carried. Construction of the Dormobile continued through until the 1990s with the company also converting vans into ambulances and minibuses. Production finally ceased in 1994.

The story of the camper van in its various guises is enormous and a bookazine such as this can only ever scratch the surface. It is hoped, however, that the content has sufficiently whetted the appetite of the reader for more information. For this reason a selection of further books and other resources can be found at the back of the book.

■ **ABOVE:** The Model T Ford helped expand people's horizons.
■ **BELOW:** A typical holiday resort as tourists visit the pier.

Development of the Camper Van

Although there had been some development of camper vans before World War 2, the major impetus to their design came in the post-war years. Although there are countless variations – particularly given the way that bespoke bodies could be added to proprietary chassis designs – there are two companies that have, perhaps, come to epitomise this type of vehicle: Volkswagen and Winnebago. The former provided the more basic model that was to become a cult vehicle during the 1960s and the latter with the massive recreational vehicles that have become so common on roads in the USA over the past 40 years. Of the two, Volkswagen has the longer history.

After the German defeat during the war, the Volkswagen factory at Wolfsburg came under British control with the damaged site under the rule of Major Ivan Hirst. Recognising the need for a basic vehicle to move materials around the factory, he created the *Plattenburg*, a flatbed vehicle based upon the chassis of the Beetle. This basic model was to inspire the figure who can, perhaps, be regarded as the true father of the Transporter, the Dutchman Ben Pon.

Pon was keen to try and develop a business importing Volkswagen vehicles into The Netherlands but the existing *Plattenwagen* did not meet required Dutch standards, chiefly because it had a driving position at the rear. In 1947 Pon produced his first sketch for a vehicle with a driving position more conventionally located at the front. However, it was not until the appointment of Heinz Heinrich Nordhoff as Volkswagen's new director general in January 1948 that serious progress was made in the development of the new model. Initially based upon the chassis of the Beetle, as had been the earlier *Plattenwagen*, work showed that using this chassis was unsuitable and, for a brief period in 1949, development was suspended. However, Nordhoff was determined to see the project progress and a modified chassis was developed; with the new chassis successfully tested, the new model was announced in mid-1949. The intention, originally, was to produce a delivery van but Nordhoff was also determined to see the model used for other purposes, such as a minibus. Following the start of production in early 1950, the vehicle had its public launch at the Geneva Motor Show.

The early model was known as the Volkswagen Type 2 or Transporter. The Type 1 was an equally iconic vehicle – the Volkswagen Beetle. Initially two versions of the Type 2 were offered: these were the Kombi (full name in German *Kombinationskraftwagen* – meaning combined-use vehicle) and the Commercial. The Kombi was designed with side windows and with detachable centre and rear seats and thus represented an ideal vehicle for conversion into a camper van. The product range was supplemented by the Microbus

■ **RIGHT:** The Berlin Motor Show of 1951, where both the VW camper van and VW Beetle took centre stage.

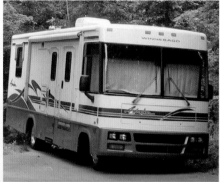

FAR LEFT: A 1947 VW Plattenwagen in a museum exhibit.

LEFT: The impressive 'Winnebago' version of a camper van.

in May 1950, the Deluxe Motorbus in June 1951 and an ambulance in December 1951. The Volkswagen was amongst the first forward-control vehicles to be produced in Europe.

Production of the first generation of the Type 2 – known as the T1 – continued through to 1967 in Germany although was to continue being built in Brazil until 1975 in near original form and 1996 in a slightly modified format. Initially work was handled at the original Volkswagen factory at Wolfsburg but was shifted in 1956 to a new facility at Hanover. Fitted with a split windscreen, the T1 was nicknamed the Splittie, the Splitscreen or Microbus. Prior to 1955, the T1 was fitted with an enormous cover over the engine at the rear; this resulted in the vehicle gaining the nickname 'Barn Door'. After 1955, the design underwent some modification and was provided with a reduced engine bay. Further modifications in 1964 saw the introduction of an optional sliding door in place of the original hinged doors that provided access to the rear section. By the time that production ceased in Germany in 1967, some 1.8 million had been constructed.

■ **ABOVE:** A splitscreen Type 2 often known as the 'splittie'.

■ **BELOW:** A typical advertisement of the time.

In 1967 came the introduction of the T2. This new model was slightly larger than the original and lost the old-style spilt windscreen. Production of this model was undertaken in Germany between 1967 and 1979 (with work at Hanover and at Emden for models for export to the USA, although the latter factory closed in the late 1970s as demand declined as a result of the fuel crisis and Japanese competition), in Mexico from 1971 to 1996, in Brazil from 1976 onwards – it remains in production here – and in Argentina from 1981 to 1986. Due to minor differences, those vehicles produced before 1971 are known as T2a and those after as T2b. A third variant – the T2c – was produced in South America; this type was fitted with a raised roof, increasing the vehicle's height by almost 10cm.

Because of the curved nature of the type's windscreen, the type has acquired the nickname 'Bay Window' or 'Bay' for short.

The T2 was replaced in 1980 by the T3, which was nicknamed 'The Wedge', and was marketed as the Vanagon in the USA. This again was larger and heavier than its predecessors and was to survive until 1990 when it was replaced by the T4, although production of the T3 continued until two years later. The T3 (also known as the T25) was the last of the models to use an air-cooled engine. This was replaced by a water-cooled engine, still located at the rear, in 1983. The T4 was to be replaced in 2003 by the T5.

The T4 Transporter, known in North America as the Eurovan, was the first of the Volkswagen models

actually to use the word 'transporter' in its name officially. It was also the first of the series to use a front-mounted engine – again, like late model T3s, this was water cooled – and was to be manufactured in both Germany and Indonesia. The type underwent a face-lift in 1994 when, in order to accommodate a larger engine, the front end of the vehicle was redesigned. As with earlier models, the T4 was a popular platform for conversion into a camper van. In the USA, Winnebago used it as the basis of the Eurovan Camper; this vehicle, which was 17 feet in length, provided sleeping accommodation for four, a cooker and a water boiler.

Launched in 2003, the Transport T5 is the most recent upgrade to the model, manufactured in Germany,

---

■ **BELOW:** A Type 2 camper van in use as an ambulance.

Poland and Indonesia. For taxation reasons, the T5 is not sold in the USA as, being classified as a light truck, it incurs a 25% tax. This tax – known as the Chicken Tax as a result of a trade dispute in the early 1960s that had severely restricted the import of Volkswagens and similar vehicles at the time (Volkswagen sales of such vehicles declined by two-thirds immediately after its

imposition) – has led manufacturers over the years to ingenious solutions to try and circumvent the restriction – with varying degrees of success (and often resulting in the loophole being closed). As a result of the tax, sales of the VW ceased in the USA following the withdrawal of the T4. Although the T5 isn't available in the USA, the conversion of the model into a motor home has adopted an

American name – the Volkswagen California. The name had been used since 1988 on products converted by Westfalia but the cessation of the relationship between Volkswagen and Westfalia resulted in the conversion work on the new version being handled in-house by Volkswagen. There are a number of models available with differing facilities: the California Beach, the California

Tramper and the California (Multivan/
Kombi) Beach. The model comes
with an elevating aluminium roof, a
sink, gas cooker, water tanks (one for
fresh and one for waste), table, chairs
and overnight accommodation.

The origins of the motor home
date back to the early 20th century

■ **ABOVE & RIGHT:** The Bay Window VW
camper van featured an optional sliding door.

■ **ABOVE:** A vintage motor home or caravan of unknown date or origin.

■ **BELOW:** An unusual modification of the T4 Transporter.

and the first dedicated clubs for the users of such vehicles date back to the 1920s. Initially many of these vehicles were simply trailers, often of relatively modest dimensions, but the real growth of the RV that is widely recognised today came in the 1950s with one name – Winnebago – perhaps coming to dominate.

Established originally in February 1958 at Forest City, Winnebago County, Iowa as an off-shoot of the Californian company Modernistic Industries, the business became known as Winnebago Industries in 1960 following the purchase of the factory by five local businessmen. The factory was initially designed to construct travel trailers but was instrumental in the development of components, such as the 'Thermo-Panel', that were to become a feature of the motor home once the first of these products rolled off the production line in 1966. The new vehicle was competitively priced – almost half the price of the competition as a result of the use of an assembly line and other manufacturing innovations – and

quickly established itself as the recreational vehicle of choice for a generation of Americans who were willing and able to spend time travelling. As with other successful products, such as Hoover, the name of a leading business – Winnebago – ultimately became synonymous with the whole product range. One identifying feature of early vehicles is the incorporation of a painted flying 'W' on the side as part of a stripe that runs from the front to the rear of the vehicle.

The name Winnebago was originally derived from a Native American tribe that inhabited the area now occupied by Iowa, Illinois and Wisconsin. As a result of this heritage, the products from the Winnebago factory until the 1980s were given Indian-based names – such as the Chief Black Hawk, the Chieftain and the Warrior.

Although generally regarded as a manufacturer of primarily larger models, the company has produced a range of smaller units over the years, with the first being the Minnie Winnie – based upon the Dodge B series – that was launched in 1973. More recently smaller units have been built upon European-supplied models. These include the 'LeSharo', based upon a Renault chassis, and the 'Rialta', which uses the Volkswagen T4 chassis as its base. In 1975 the company launched another product range under the brand name Itasca and a third brand, ERA, was added in 2008 to supply Class B vehicles.

After 20 years of production, in 1986, the company produced its 200,000th RV; the milestone of 400,000 units was reached 22 years later. In 2004 12,500 units were produced and Winnebago has held the position of number one manufacturer of Class A and C motor homes annually since 2001.

As a result of a steep drop in demand, one of the company's manufacturing plants, at Charles City, was closed in 2008 although this site has subsequently reopened partially. The factors behind the closure were symptomatic of the decline in consumer confidence in the wake of the banking crisis and the lack of available finance. Another contributory factor – and one that is likely to affect the demand for such RVs in the future – is the overall increase in the cost of fuel. US citizens have been used to relatively low fuel costs over many years; as the price of fuels has increased dramatically over recent years so the cost of running these gas-guzzling vehicles has also risen.

The 2011 range for Winnebago includes seven Class A models – with names such as Journey, Journey Express and Sightseer – with four Class C models – with names such as Aspect and View Profile. The most expensive unit, the Class A Tour will set customers back a cool $330,000.

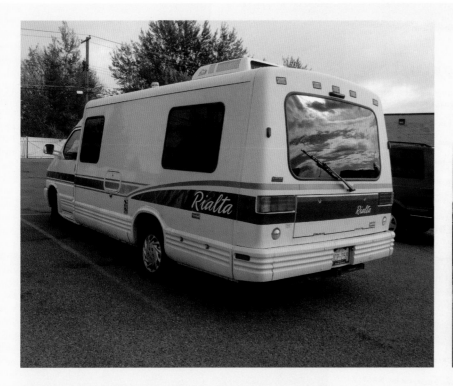

■ **ABOVE:** The Winnebago Rialta RV based upon the VW T4 camper van.

■ **ABOVE RIGHT:** A poster in Winnebago illustrating the company's products.

■ **LEFT:** The more recent T4 Transporter.

Travelling by Camper Van

In the early 1960s one of the British-produced conversions, made by Canterbury Pitt, was marketed with the following spiel: 'Go anywhere – see everything, free from timetable restrictions and accommodation problems. No hotel bills for your family and friends… there's plenty of room for all… with your gear neatly stowed away in the ample locker and wardrobe space. Be free as a bird to wander as the mood takes you, stopping at will. Or, when not on pleasure bent turn your caravan in to a highly mobile office. The furniture swings into several self-locking arrangements with remarkable ease, or folds away to increase the low central floor space to 16sq ft so that your caravan

■ **BELOW:** Travelling on the open road in camper van style.

■ **BELOW LEFT:** Advertising the Devon Caravette.

February 10, 1960   The Motor

LOOK AT THIS FOR VALUE!

THE DEVON 'CARAVETTE'

The Devon "Caravette" undoubtedly offers the very finest value for your money – built by Devon craftsmen, the materials used and the excellent workmanship conform to the highest standard. The "Caravette" is a car, and at the same time a caravan – a mobile 'home – an office – it has so many uses! Converted from the famous VW microbus there is all-round independent suspension, heater, spare wheel, trafficators, bench seat – all included in price.

LICENSED AS A CAR - NO PURCHASE TAX

* THE DUAL-PURPOSE VEHICLE
* ELECTRIC & GAS LIGHTING
* FORMICA SURFACES
* DEEP FOAM UPHOLSTERY
* SOLID OAK FITTINGS
  Full set of crockery for 4 people, "Easicool" food storage cabinet and 4-gallon water container.
* 3 MODELS AVAILABLE
  £910 to **£930**

Designed and produced by J. P. WHITE LTD. of Sidmouth, Devon.
Distributed by LISBURNE GARAGE, Babbacombe Road, Torquay, Devon
●
SOLE CONCESSIONAIRES FOR THE VOLKSWAGEN IN THE UNITED KINGDOM
VW MOTORS LTD., Lord's Court, 32/34 St. John's Wood Road, London, N.W.8

Please send me without obligation the fully illustrated brochure on the Devon "Caravette".

Post this coupon today to VW Motors Ltd.

NAME ....

ADDRESS ....

becomes a willing work horse for the transport of bulky packages.' If the experience of travelling with a camper van can be epitomised into a single paragraph, then that advertising text perhaps encapsulates it. Ultimately everything about the camper van or motor home can be encompassed by a single word – freedom.

The promotional material created to advertise the various conversions available reflected this to a considerable extent. In the mid-1970s the Devon Caravette was advertised with the following: 'Our camper is not just a camper. It's whatever you want it to be… When other cars finish this VW begins. It

---

■ **RIGHT:** The Canterbury Pitt advert.

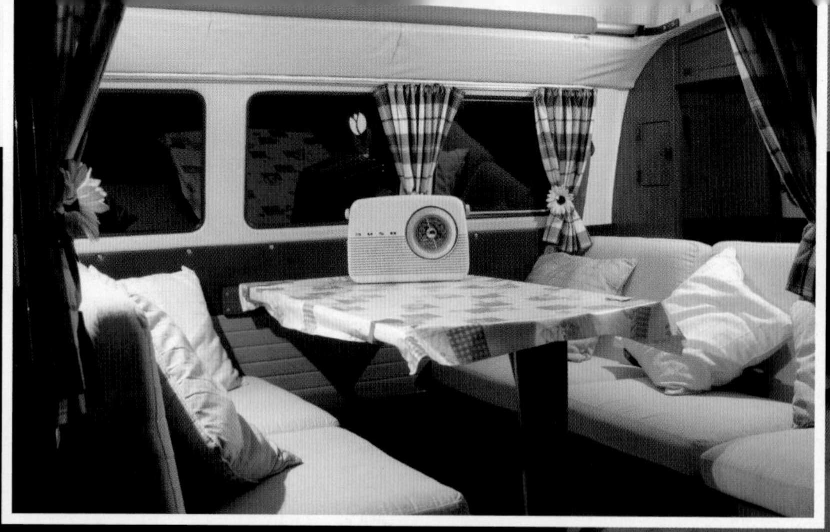

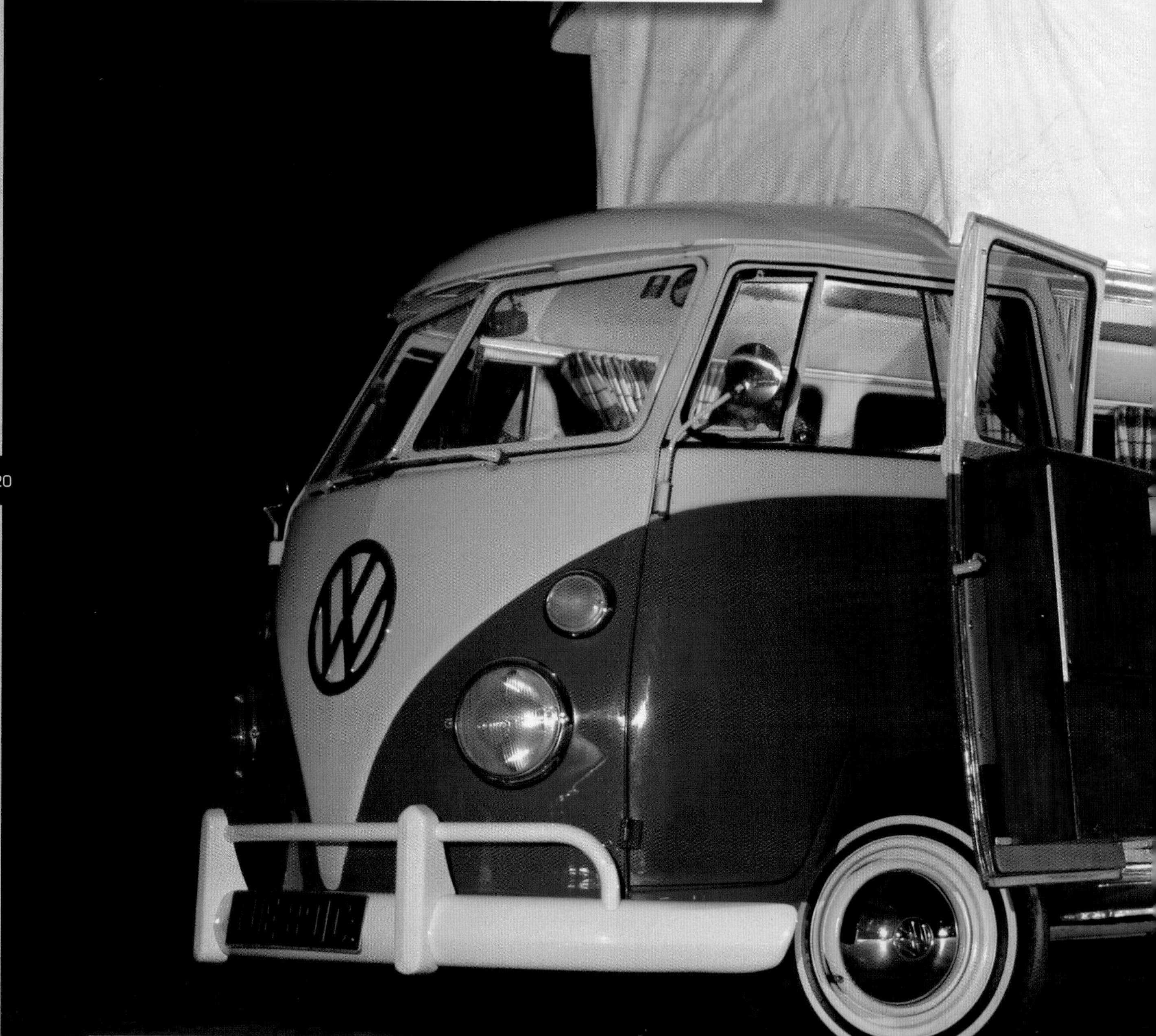

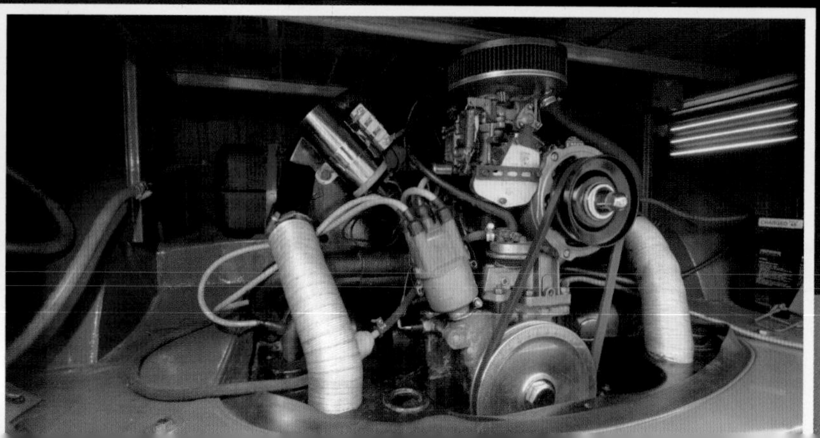

can be your English country cottage or your villa in some sun-drenched foreign part. And unlike any cottage or villa you can pack up and go, anywhere you like… Truly a car for all occasions.'

Almost from the start travellers realised the potential that the camper van offered for experiencing far-flung places. In 1952 one of the earliest of the Westfalia conversions was displayed at the Frankfurt Motor Show. The vehicle was bought after the show by Helmut and Erna Blenck who used it to traverse South Africa the following year. Two years later, in 1955, they related the story of their journey in the book *South Africa Today: A Travel Book*. Their text reflected the freedom that the camper van offered over the conventional car, commenting 'This time we were able to do what we had long planned: use a car that enabled us to cover great distances in comfort and stop for the night just when we wanted, quite independent of towns and hotels. But even more important than the possibility of sleeping in the car was the convenient way in which we were able to carry all our luggage.' Amongst other aspects highlighted by the Blencks were the vehicle's reliability and its ability to cope with the worst terrain that the country was able to offer.

If there is another word that epitomises the traveller's experience of driving the Volkswagen camper van in particular and other models more generally then that word is reliability. The Volkswagen's air-cooled engine proved to be highly successful in getting travellers to their destination, coping easily with the high temperatures to be encountered on the 'Hippie trail' to India, for example, provided that the engine oil and the dust filters were regularly

■ **LEFT:** Inside and out of a beautifully restored T2 splitscreen VW camper van.

checked and replaced. Moreover when there was a problem, the technology was such that repairs were easily made.

The Winnebago and similar models were generally much larger than other camper vans and, whilst ideal perhaps to the wide open spaces of North America, were possibly less well suited to the narrower and more confined road space of the old world. Despite this, the ownership of these types of vehicle has grown significantly in Europe over the past 30 years.

The camper van was ideal as a means of transporting the family from home to a chosen destination; in many cases, however, once based at the campsite or other resort, one of the limitations of the van became self-evident – once established as part of the camp (with roof raised and awnings extended) the van was no longer available as a means of transport. From a relatively early period this problem was overcome by the use of cycle racks but as vehicles have grown bigger and more powerful so the options available to users have grown. It is now possible to see camper vans regularly towing trailers – and many of these, such as the cut-down Volkswagen Beetle, are just as customised as the actual van – and, with the most powerful of the Winnebago-style motor homes it is even possible to tow a secondary car behind. Thus the main van can be left deposited at its parking site whilst its owners have complete flexibility to travel around the country in the second vehicle.

■ **RIGHT:** Selling the holiday lifestyle.

■ **LEFT & BELOW:** Enjoying a holiday Winnebago style.

March 2, 1960

26 The Motor

You'll be comfortably 'at home' in the

COMMER 2-4 berth CARAVAN
PETROL OR DIESEL POWERED

WHETHER you're off for a day in the country or a holiday by the sea this fine new Commer Caravan has everything to make you delightfully, comfortably, 'at home'.

It provides accommodation for up to four persons; there are cupboards for everything you need; a roomy wardrobe; a fully-equipped kitchen with gas cooker; a sink unit; bright interior decorations, and a three-seat driver's compartment.

The basis of this attractive, factory-produced vehicle of all-steel unitary construction is the new Commer ¾ tonner with easily-accessible power unit, petrol or diesel; independent front suspension; silent synchromesh gearbox; hypoid rear axle, and 'easy-ride' rear springing.

Full details on request from your local Commer dealer.

By day, a four-seat 'dinette'.   At night, a two or four-berth bedroom.   Gas cooker and sink unit.

A ROOTES PRODUCT — BUILT STRONGER TO LAST LONGER!

COMMER CARS LIMITED LUTON BEDFORDSHIRE   EXPORT DIVISION: ROOTES LIMITED DEVONSHIRE HOUSE PICCADILLY LONDON W.1
R20

The Campsite Experience

For users of camper vans and larger motor homes, the experience of the campsite inevitably varied upon the type of vehicle used and the facilities that it offered. Initially, these facilities were severely limited – often simply the provision of a pack that enabled the rear compartment of the van to be used as a basic sleeping or eating area. Thus the user needed a fully-fledged campsite to provide more significant facilities, such as running water, sanitation and showers. One of the concomitant developments to that of the camper van from the 1950s onwards was also the development of the campsite. The popularity of camping had grown up from the post-World War 1 generation but it was again the boom in leisure time and the provision of paid holidays that enabled more to experience this type of trip.

In looking at the lifestyle associated with the camper van, one thing must

be noted and that is the fact that the vast majority of vehicles were not purpose-built as camper vans but were conversions of vehicles, normally light commercial vehicles, by manufacturers other than those who had constructed the original vehicle. Whilst companies like Volkswagen produced many thousands of vans, companies like Dormobile and Danbury provided conversions that were, to a certain extent, bespoke. Whilst the basic conversion would probably include increasing the interior's height by some form of lifting roof and the provision of basic facilities, the ultimate customer could add to these facilities depending on taste and budget. Thus each vehicle was slightly different and so each user's experiences of using the camper would also be subtly different.

Many of the conversions to the proprietary vans included awnings or tent extensions that could be fitted to the outside of the van and which, therefore, extended the accommodation offered by the van. As such the camper was almost little more than a means of transport.

■ **ABOVE:** A perfect evening in a readymade campsite!

Een practische familiewagen (steeds)   **en een rijdend hotel (soms)**

Welk ouderpaar zou daar nog niet van hebben gedroomd? Een auto voor het hele gezin met alles wat daarbij hoort. Meer nog: een rollend huis op wielen – alleen veel, veel goedkoper als een normaal zomerhuisje. Deze „droom"-wagen ziet u hier. Daarin kunt u allen meenemen: vrouw en kinderen, grootouders of de buren.

Al het andere kunt u ook meenemen: koffers, pakjes, tassen, hengels, tenten, het hobbelpaard, sportuitrusting – wat u maar wilt. U kunt weekend uitstapjes ondernemen of met vacantie gaan – met uw familie of met vrienden of kennissen. Voor allen is er ruimschoots plaats. Vaak ook is de wagen een hotel op wielen. Dus uw eetkamer, woonkamer of slaapkamer.

Met kastjes voor de kleren en de keukenuitrusting. Met een isolatiebox en een drinkwaterreservoir. Met vriendelijke gordijntjes en een (afneembare) hanglamp. Met zitbanken, die 's-avonds in twee slaapplaatsen voor volwassenen veranderd worden. (Kleine Hans en de jongste telg slapen in een stabiel hangbed). Met een luifeltent, die als strandcabine of als terras-

afscheiding – met schaduw – kan dienen. Hoe die verandering in een „camping-villa" plaats vindt? Heel eenvoudig en snel. U neemt de zitbanken er uit en zet de kampeerset voor de VW-bus erin. Uit de inbouwset kunt u naar wens uw eigen „mobile zomerhuisje" samenstellen: ieder onderdeel kunt u apart in- en uitbouwen. U zult veel plezier van zo'n bouwdoos hebben. Uw hele gezin raakt al van te voren in de vacantiestemming.

- **ABOVE:** Camping Sixties style.
- **RIGHT:** A Dormobile conversion offered extra luxuries.

One of the great beauties of the camper van was that it offered secure accommodation; this was particularly useful in inclement weather when conventional tents might easily fail and leave the occupants drenched. Numerous camper van users narrate stories of being happily ensconced in their van overnight, oblivious to the raging storm outside, only to wake up the following morning to discover that the rest of the campsite was a picture of destruction and very wet and cold campers.

When first introduced, the Westfalia conversion kit was relatively rudimentary. The standard equipment included a laminated

folding table, curtains, water tank and pump, cold box and various folding seats. Additional, but optional equipment included a portable chemical toilet, a camping stove, side tents and awnings. The Dormobile, first introduced in 1957, was better appointed from new in that it included a cooker and sink. This was, however, a reflection of the fact that, under British tax regulations, provided the vehicle was fitted with equipment that was deemed 'built-in life support equipment', the vehicles were deemed to be free of Purchase Tax, which was, at that stage, only imposed on passenger cars.

The lack of facilities thus required access to sites that could provide them. The campsite was one option but as the popularity of caravanning increased alongside the growth in the use of camper vans and RVs so a network of caravan parks has grown up in Europe, Australia and North America. Some of these sites see semi-permanent occupation, whilst others cater for a more itinerant population but all provide the essential services that users of such vehicles require. These will include at the most basic fresh water and sewage, but the more sophisticated will also offer convenience stores, swimming pools and a whole range of other attractions. Just as the vehicles themselves have got more sophisticated over the years, so too have the facilities on offer at these sites. The scale of the business can be gauged from the fact that the Camping & Caravanning Club has over 400,000 members and operates more than 100 sites in the United Kingdom.

Obviously, as the facilities on the vehicles themselves become more sophisticated, and this is particularly true of the massive all-singing all-dancing RVs, so the need for land-based facilities is replaced by a simple need for a place to be able to park legally overnight. Inevitably, the USA has a vast number of sites aimed at the RV market, again with varying levels of facility on offer; the largest chain of such facilities is operated by a company called Kampgrounds of America. A reflection of the increasing presence of the recreational vehicle in Europe is the growth, over the past 30 years, of a network of RV parking sites. These are known as Aire de Camping-car in France and Reisenmobil-Stellplatz in Germany.

■ **BELOW:** Some of the facilities on board a VW camper van after conversion.

Everyday Life

In many respects the Volkswagen Kombi was an ideal vehicle for the development of the camper van in that being designed so that the rear compartment could be converted easily into an alternative use at weekends, the model was ideal for workaday use during the week and for leisure come holidays.

The lifestyle associated with the RV is very different to that experienced by the use of the traditional camper van. This is a reflection of the range of facilities available on the RVs as well as the profile of many of the users. Inevitably, the various types of user have acquired nicknames as a result of their use of the RV. One particularly common aspect of the RV lifestyle is its adoption by the elderly; many of these will sell up their conventional home and invest in a mobile home

that enables them to migrate to warmer climes in the winter. In Australia this ageing population of travellers is known as 'grey nomads' whilst in the USA the habit of migrating south in the winter to states like Florida before returning north in the spring is known as 'snowbirding'.

Other groups are known as 'fulltimers' – these are people who have opted to live permanently in their RV – and 'workampers' – who are people who use their RV as a base whilst working in the same camp. The rise of modern technology – in particular the internet and mobile telephony – has increasingly allowed for people to work from their motor home whilst travelling the country.

CAMPER VANs AND RVs

No longer does the breadwinner need to be tied to a specific location; the combination of technology and the RV has provided the current generation of motor home users with a lifestyle that would have seemed impossible only 20 years ago.

The RV has become a vehicle of choice for many famous Americans from the world of sport, entertainment and even politics. Amongst these stars are Barack Obama, US Supreme Court Justice Clarence Thomas, Pamela Anderson, Dolly Parton, Colin Farrell, Sean Penn, the late Paul Newman, Robert De Niro, Bode Miller, David Letterman, George Foreman and Davis Love. The factors behind the choice are multifarious but often revolve around the freedom, the flexibility and even the nostalgia for road trips in their youth. According to De Niro 'Airline travel being what it is these days – so unreliable – I'll feel much more comfortable knowing I have my own posturepedic bed; my own thermostat; my own lavatory facility' whilst fellow actor Rob Lowe noted 'My kids love riding about in these big RVs – like an old-fashioned road trip like when I was a kid'. Another actor, Jeff Daniels, who appeared with Robin Williams in the film *RV Runaway Vacation* and who currently owns a Gulf Steam Tour Master, commented on the freedom that the RV offered when he noted 'I love seeing parts of the country

BELOW: Grey nomads making the most of their retirement.

I wouldn't otherwise [see]', a view echoed by another actor, Matthew McConaughey who referred to 'The freedom of being able to pull up, stop, power up anywhere you want – beach or whatever. Setup and have your front yard different every single day'. Even when he's at home McConaughey sometimes prefers to use his RV. 'It's one of my favourite places. I've got a house but even when I pull into my house, sometimes I sleep in that thing in my driveway. It's really comfortable.' For sportsmen, the RV is often the ideal form of transport as it enables them to keep all their kit together in one place. The golfer Davis Love noted his preference for an RV: 'Having all your clothes in the motor home and not having to pack suitcases, you can get used to that. Plus we can take our motorcycle.'

One of the social groups that took to the camper van in a massive way was the surfing fraternity initially in the USA and Australia. The vehicle offered an ideal means of carrying all the gear associated with the sport and over the years this relationship has continued to grow. Surfing itself has become much more international and the close relationship between the sport and the camper van is still evident today.

Amongst the most prominent of the surfers who made great use of the camper van is Dorian 'Doc' Paskowitz. A native of Texas and a trained doctor – hence the nickname – Paskowitz and his family have become known as the 'First family of surfing'. In the late 1950s, after a period in Israel, Paskowitz and his third wife adopted a highly bohemian lifestyle, living in a series of camper vans with their ever-increasing family (eventually the couple had nine children in all) whilst Paskowitz himself worked as a professional surfer. The family's story was related in the documentary film *Surfwise*,

■ **ABOVE:** Selling the lifestyle.

■ **BELOW:** Planning a route for that perfect break.

■ **ABOVE & RIGHT:**
Relative luxury on board
a typical RV.

which was written and directed by Doug Pray. Perhaps reflecting the unorthodox lifestyle of its proponents, the film was marketed with the strap line 'Reject Normal!' and featured one of the family's numerous camper vans on the poster.

In Britain, the undoubted surfing centre of the country is Cornwall with Newquay and the surrounding area amongst the most popular of destinations. Every year, the link between the camper van and surfing is reflected in the Run to the Sun – www.runtothesun.co.uk – event that draws countless enthusiasts for three

■ **ABOVE:** Parked and ready to enjoy a holiday.

days to the Cornish resort each May. First established in 1987, when 70 vehicles participated, the event has grown exponentially over the years.

The Run to the Sun is but one of a whole range of festivals held annually in Britain and overseas that celebrate the camper van culture. Some of these are dedicated to individual marques – most notably the Volkswagen – but others just celebrate the culture of the camper

van more generally. Other notable festivals in Britain include the Big Bang Camper & Bus Show (www.big-bang.co.uk), the British Volkswagen Festival (www.bvwf.co.uk), Volksfest (a number of regional events held annually in the UK and overseas, these include Plymouth [www.plymouthvolksfest.co.uk], Bristol [www.bristolvolksfest.co.uk], Wales [www.volksfestwales.org.uk] and London [www.vwaction.com/vwlvf]),

VW Action (www.vwaction.co.uk), Wight Aircooled (wightcooledvws.proboards.com/index.cgi), Vanfest (www.vanfest.org) and VW Festival (www.vwfestival.co.uk). These events draw countless enthusiasts together to celebrate their shared interest in Volkswagens and represent an ideal opportunity to further one's own interest in the subject.

Another increasingly popular aspect of the camper van lifestyle is vehicle restoration. Given that the story of the Westfalia conversion of the Volkswagen Kombi now stretches back some six decades and the proprietary conversions of Volkswagens and other models can stretch back almost as long, many of these vehicles have now reached a 'classic' status with the result that the second-hand and restoration market has grown in importance. The beauty of a conversion is that, provided that the basic vehicle is in reasonable condition (and even if it isn't the parts are generally available to restore it), it is possible to obtain many of the traditional fixtures and fittings either new or in a reconditioned state. Many of these restorations can be seen at the numerous rallies that are held and information about obtaining second-hand vehicles and their restoration can be found easily through the various message boards and forums of like-minded individuals on the Internet. Moreover, many of the original manufacturers remain in business and, conscious of the interest in these older vehicles, ensure that the relevant equipment and fittings remain available.

Like many special interest groups,

users of camper vans are inevitably involved in fund-raising both for their own societies and for other charities. Derived directly from the appearance of a camper van in the classic 1969 film *Alice's Restaurant*, in which the career of the musician Arlo Guthrie was recorded and his father, Guthrie, was shown suffering from Huntingdon's Disease (from which he later died), from 2001 an annual walk – the Guthrie Walk – has been held in Massachusetts to raise funds to support those suffering from this debilitating illness. Over the past decade many thousands of dollars have been raised with the walkers being transported in old Volkswagens. In Britain, the Mustard Seed Ministries was set up as a charity in 1993 to raise funds for Indian street children; the charity uses a camper van to attend VW rallies and other events across the UK. These are but two of the many causes that camper van users worldwide support.

33

■ **BELOW:** Easy accessibility to the beach for this Commer.

The Hippie Lifestyle

The 1960s represented for many a decade of comparative freedom and tolerance; a lot of the accepted social mores were in decline and levels of prosperity had increased. Although the world was not a wholly stable society – as evinced by the threat of nuclear war narrowly averted after the Cuban missile crisis – and there remained the threat, particularly later in the

decade, of the draft for a generation of young American men as the Vietnam War became an ever more voracious monster that required feeding, for many – particularly the young – the years were ones where sex, drugs and Rock and Roll were to be experienced.

It was from this era that the Hippie movement emerged. Initially developing in the USA in the early 1960s – the name is derived from the word *hipster* referring to the beatniks (itself derived from the beat generation in combination with *sputnik*) who were starting to congregate in specific urban areas such as Greenwich Village in New York – the subculture represented by the Hippies gradually spread worldwide, encouraged by contemporary music – such as the psychedelic rock popularised by Jimi Hendrix – and by the availability of drugs such as LSD. The era witnessed the boom in music festivals – such as the first Isle of Wight Festival of 1968 – and the concept of free love, but by the end of the decade the Manson murders and

■ **BELOW:** The birth of the Hippie lifestyle.

many of the excesses shown at the great festivals saw a gradual waning of the movement as new trends – such as Punk in the mid-1970s – emerged. In some respects, however, many of the mores of the Hippie movement were gradually to become more mainstream as the Hippie generation itself aged.

One of the most important facets of the Hippie lifestyle was travel and it was into this mien that the VW in particular was to prove its worth as a vehicle for the counterculture. A variety of vehicles were used by the Hippies but amongst the most popular was undoubtedly the VW as it enabled a group to travel together cheaply. The availability of cheap used models was also an advantage. Frequently repainted in a customised style and with a peace symbol often replacing the VW logo, the Volkswagen was a familiar site at all of the great Hippie festivals. Travelling light, the Hippie often moved from site to site as they were drawn to new festivals, to the increasingly common anti-Vietnam War demonstrations or simply because the 'vibes' were wrong. For those who decided against hitch-hiking – another preferred method of getting around the country – the VW was integral to this lifestyle.

The ability of the VW to move across the country cheaply was also recognised by those within the Hippie community that wished to travel further afield. Organisations such as European Adventure and Student Travel were established in the late 1960s to facilitate group holidays on the cheap to Europe. Based around a group of VWs running in convoy, these trips could last up to two months and were hugely popular amongst college students of the era. Another aspect of the Hippie lifestyle was the almost mythical trek to India. Again, the Volkswagen and other such camper vans represented an

■ **ABOVE:** The Hippie lifestyle and camper in perfect harmony.

■ **TOP RIGHT:** The Woodstock Festival and Vanfest logo made up from campers.

■ **LEFT:** On show!

ideal means of transport. Rugged and reliable, they were easily maintained if the need arose and were sufficiently capacious to allow a group with their belongings to make the journey.

The scale of the Hippie lifestyle at its peak was enormous; the Woodstock Festival held at Bethel, New York, in August 1969, drew some half-a-million people to the event. Many of these would have travelled there by Volkswagen.

The Camper Van on Screen

As a result of its longevity, its association with the alternative culture of
the 1960s and the great range of customisation to which the models have
been subject, the various types of Volkswagen camper van have appeared
in numerous films and TV programmes over the years. In terms of film
appearances, these include the 2006 movie *Little Miss Sunshine* in which a
yellow and white second generation Volkswagen is driven by the family from
New Mexico to California to enable the daughter to appear in the finals of a
beauty pageant. The film's poster also included an image of the van. Other
classic film appearances include the aforementioned *Alice's Restaurant*
(1969), directed by Arthur Penn in which the songwriter Arlo Guthrie travels
widely using his 1964 camper, *Field of Dreams* (1989), in which Kevin Costner

ABOVE: A 'Kombi' as mentioned in the Men at Work song *Down Under*.

uses a VW to travel cross-country in order to kidnap James Earl Jones, and *Forrest Gump* (1994), directed by Robert Zemeckis and starring Tom Hanks, in which Jenny Curran (played by Robin Wright) is seen getting out of a VW while living the Hippie lifestyle at the time that Gump was in Vietnam. Starring Robert Downey Jr and Kiefer Sutherland, the 1988 film *1969* directed by Ernest Thompson chronicles the life of two young men from small-town America at the height of the Vietnam War and the opposition to the draft. The protagonists make use of an early Volkswagen split-windscreen vehicle that's painted in a Hippie

BELOW: The famous camper van.

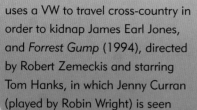

40

CAMPER VANs AND RVs

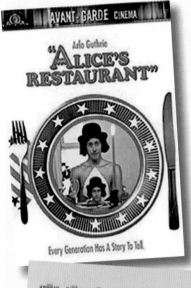

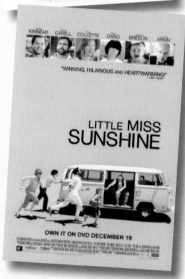

■ **ABOVE:** Jamie Oliver used a camper van in his show *Jamie's Great Italian Escape*.

style. In terms of documentary film, the classic has undoubtedly got to be the three-hour film *Woodstock* that was directed by Michael Wadleigh. The film is a detailed chronicle of the festival. The central role of the Volkswagen to the Hippie culture is demonstrated graphically in the account of the concert. Another documentary – the yet to be released *Art Officially Favored* written and directed by Martin Yernazian – features the street musician Michael Masley, who is world renowned for the use of his bowhammers technique on the cymbalom. Masley lives in a camper and the vehicle, which broke down frequently during the period that the film took to shoot, appears regularly through the film.

Although not strictly featuring an actual camper van, the animated film *Father Christmas*, based upon two of Raymond Briggs' illustrated books for children and directed by Dave Unwin, has Father Christmas undertaking the conversion of his sleigh into a camper van for a holiday following his one working day of the year. His trip takes him to France, Scotland and North America. The UK version of the film had a voice-over by the comedian Mel Smith.

In terms of appearances on television, the Volkswagen again has a number of credits to its name. In an episode of *Law & Order – Ramparts* originally broadcast in January 1999 – the plot revolves around a Volkswagen being recovered from the Hudson River with the body of a college radical from 30 years earlier being found within the recovered vehicle. Another notable television appearance was on the BBC's motoring programme *Top Gear*, broadcast originally in May 2006, when Richard Hammond attempted to convert a Volkswagen T3 into an amphibious vehicle. The conversion, however, proved unsuccessful as it sank into a reservoir in the Peak

■ **ABOVE:** The amphibious converted camper as used by Richard Hammond on *Top Gear*.

District as a result of structural problems and a broken propeller. On British television, the celebrity chef Jamie Oliver, a noted camper van enthusiast, used a 1959 Volkswagen camper van for his television series *Jamie's Great Italian Escape*. The six-part Channel 4 series, broadcast originally in 2005, featured the chef driving round Italy in the blue and white van as he sampled the nation's culinary delights. Apart from Jamie Oliver, other celebrity owners of the camper van include the actor Martin Clunes, the creator of 'Wallace & Gromit' Nick Parks, the actor Wilhelm von Homburg and the Formula One racing driver Jenson Button. One well-known owner of a Bedford-based Dormobile was the author Anthony Burgess, who used it to travel widely in the late 1960s. Although he enjoyed the vehicle he was less impressed with its quality; he commented that the vehicle was 'a miracle of British design, although much let down by shoddy British execution – screws missing [and] bad wood-planing'.

A camper van also makes an appearance in several episodes of the cult BBC series *Being Human* as the home of Thomas MacNair (played by Michael Socha), a young werewolf, and his adopted father, Anthony Michael MacNair (played by Robson Green), a fellow werewolf and vampire hunter. The pair appeared in four episodes – *The Wolf-Shaped Bullet*, *Though the Heavens Fall*, *The*

Pack and *Lie* – that were originally broadcast in early 2011. Another, but earlier, appearance was in the Channel 4 soap opera *Brookside* devised by Phil Redmond. One of the characters in the series, Barry Grant (played by Paul Usher), had a penchant for cars of various types but, relatively early in the programme's run in the late 1980s, having been forced out of the family home, Grant was forced to live rough for a period in a Volkswagen Camper. Another Channel 4 soap opera originally conceived by Phil Redmond

is *Hollyoaks*, a series about the life and times of students at a community college. In 2010 a number of the characters, having been thwarted in their efforts to get to a music festival by only having photocopied tickets, decide to go on tour, travelling to France in a camper van.

Outside film and television, the Volkswagen has also appeared in the video game *Grand Theft Auto: San Andreas*. One of the characters in the game, a hippie called Truth, possesses a camper called *The Mothership*. There are at least five

popular songs that also include reference to the Volkswagen. In 1967, before the release of the film with the same name, the Arlo Guthrie single *Alice's Restaurant* was released and made reference to a 'red VW microbus'. It is believed that The Who track *Magic Bus*, written by Peter Townsend in 1965 but not actually released until three years later, features a camper although the sleeve of the record actually features a more conventional elderly British double-deck bus (albeit painted in a psychedelic colour scheme). The Bruce Springsteen album *Greetings from Ashbury Park NJ*, released in 1973, includes the track *The Angel* in which the following line – 'Volkswagen vans with full running boards driving great anchors' – appears. In 1976 C W McCall (the pseudonym of William D Fries) released *Convoy* at the height of the craze for Citizens' Band radio; this record, which was his most popular release selling more than two million copies, included the line 'eleven long-haired friends of Jesus in a chartreuse microbus'. Like *Alice's Restaurant*, *Convoy* was also to be filmed – in 1978 – for which McCall provided a revised version of the original song. The film was directed by Sam Peckinpah and starred Kris Kristofferson and Ali Macgraw. In

■ **BELOW:** The Who track *Magic Bus* was believed to have been based on a camper van, the band later had this specially sprayed for a competition.

44

1982 the single *Down Under* by Men at Work made reference to 'Travelling in a fried-out Kombi, On the hippie trail, head full of zombie'.

Given the almost iconic status of the Winnebago in North American life, it's inevitable that the RV has appeared in a number of films over the years. These films include the Disney classic *Escape to Witch Mountain* (1975), which starred Eddie Albert, Ray Milland and Donald Pleasance alongside a 1974 Winnebago Minnie. Other films include John Landis' *The Blues Brothers* (1980), starring Dan Akroyd and John Belushi, Mel Brooks' comedy *Spaceballs* (1987), Jeremiah Chechik's *National Lampoon's Christmas Vacation* (1989), in which the Griswald family's plans for the Festive Season go sadly awry, Alexander Payne's *About Schmidt* (2002), starring Jack Nicholson, and Jay Roach's *Meet the Fockers* (2004), starring Robert De Niro, Ben Stiller and Dustin Hoffman. In the 2006 film *RV: Runaway Vacation* directed by Barry Sonnenfeld, Robin Williams stars as Bob Munro, a harassed executive who hires an RV for a family trip with his wife and two children to the Colorado Rockies. Marketed with the strap line 'On a family vacation no one can here you scream', the film's poster included an RV balanced precariously – and impossibly – on top of a mountain!

A type of camper van is central to the classic Jacques Tati film *Trafic* of 1971. In the film, Tati, as the accident-prone Monsieur Hulot, designs an ingenious camper van for a small and struggling French car company. The plot revolves around getting the prototype of the vehicle from the factory for display at the Amsterdam Motor Show. Inevitably, there are countless incidents en route – including a superbly choreographed road accident – that delay the vehicle's journey to the show.

Although not a film as yet (but it can only be a matter of time), it has been announced that the author Frank Cottrell Boyce has been authorised by the family of Ian Fleming to write a sequel to the classic children's story *Chitty Chitty Bang Bang*. The original novel, which was filmed in 1968 starring Dick Van Dyke, Lionel Jeffries and Sally Ann Howes, featured a vintage sports car with magical powers. The sequel to the original novel will feature a family whose life is turned upside down when they decide to replace the original engine in their camper van with an engine salvaged from an old racing car.

Apart from the appearance of the camper van in film, there are also at least two fact-based television series devoted to the genre of camper vans and caravanning: the first of these is *Caravans: A British Love Affair*, which was fronted by Alison Steadman, and the second is *One Man and his Camper Van*, a series of 10 programmes in which Martin Dorey travels the length and breadth of the country in his camper van. These were both shown on the BBC and further details can be found via the BBC website: www.bbc.co.uk. There was also the documentary, *Winnebago Man*, produced in 2010 that featured an RV salesman called Jack Rebney, who shot to fame following the appearance of the out-takes from a sales video dating to 1989 on the Internet.

The iconic status of the camper van has also been reflected in at least two adverts in Britain. In 2007, Marks & Spencer used a light-blue 'Bay' camper van, which was portrayed being driven to the beach whilst, in 2011, the Spanish bank Santander – as the new owners of various British financial institutions – created a red T1 through the use of Lego-style bricks to promote its services.

■ **ABOVE:** A 'Kombi' as featured in both song and movie.

45

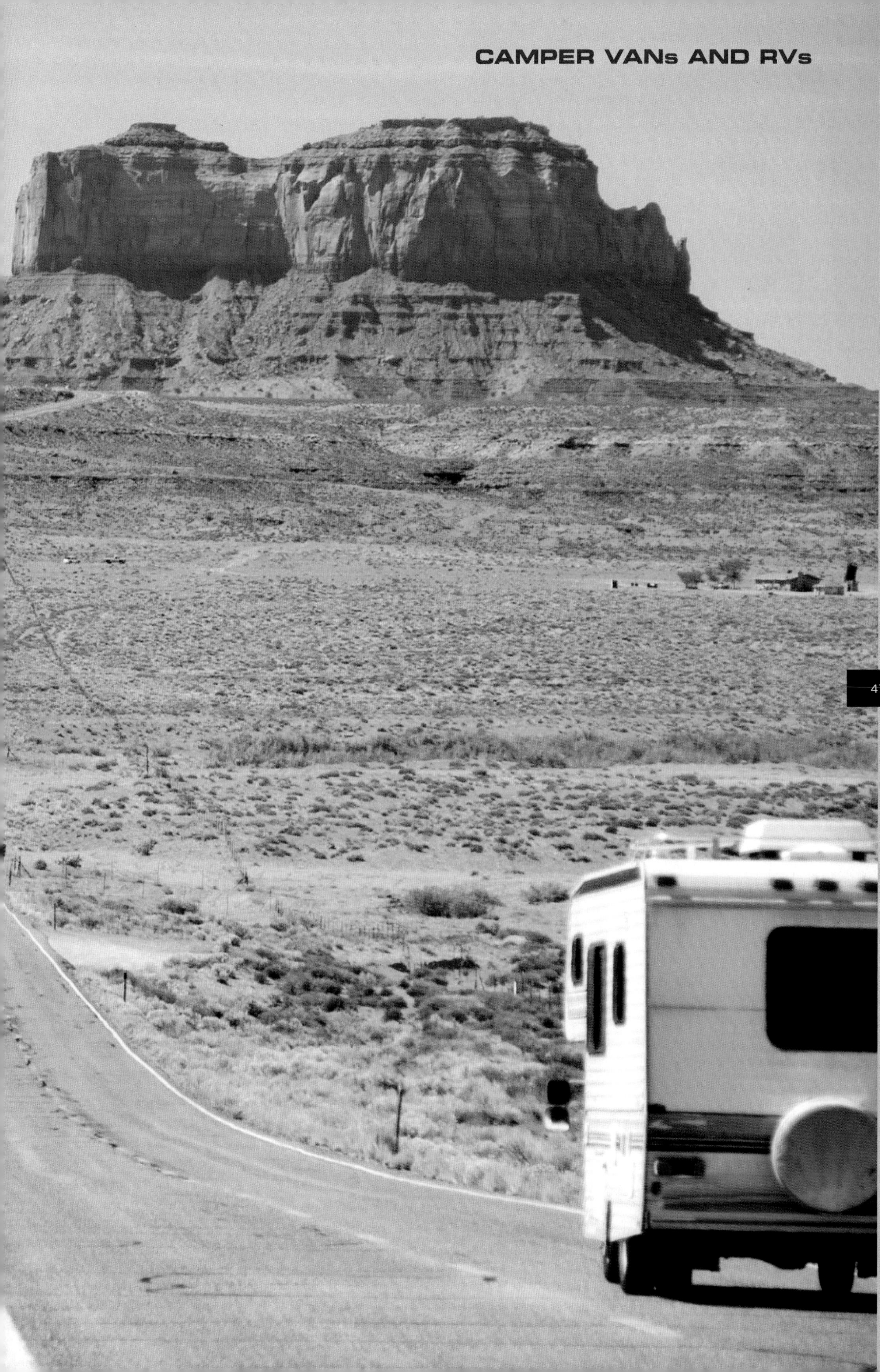

48

Customisation and Conversions

THE VOLKSWAGEN CARAVETTE...

NO HOTEL WORRIES
NO COSTLY TRAVEL
NO LOST TIME
NO TOWING PROBLEMS
NO PURCHASE TAX

Sole distributors of Volkswagen for Hampshire and Dorset.

MODERN LIGHT CARS LTD

110/112 Lodge Road, Southampton
Tel: Southampton 22828
318 Holdenhurst Road, Bournemouth
Tel: Bourn......33304

BE FREE AS A GIPSY

AND ENJOY LIFE IN A

DEVON

CARAVETTE

To go where you like—when you like. Independence that puts the world at your feet—in the luxury of superb comfort.

★ Converted from the famous Volkswagen Microbus. All round independent suspension.
★ Air cooled rear engine, always starts promptly, cannot freeze or boil.
★ Weather proof finish, built in heater, spare wheel and other "extras" included in the price.
★ A car or caravan for a family of four. An office or a mobile home.
★ Exceptional value at £945. No Purchase Tax.

SPECIAL INSURANCE RATES FOR VOLKSWAGEN VEHICLES.

Post this coupon to-day to Volkswagen

NAME
ADDRESS

Designed and produced by J.P. WHITE LTD. of Sidmouth, Devon

Distributed by
LISBURNE GARAGE
BABBACOMBE ROAD, TORQUAY, DEVON

VOLKSWAGEN 32-34 St. John's Wood Road, London, N.W.8. 'Phone: CUNningham 8000 West End Showrooms: 38-39 Stratton St., London, W.1. Phone GROsvenor 4666

Over the years the camper van has been subject to many modifications; some of these have been produced in significant numbers, whilst others have been one-offs created by individuals to reflect their own needs and interests. To a certain extent, given the fact that many of the most widely available camper vans were custom-built on proprietary vehicle chassis, customisation was almost the norm.

One of the earliest and most important of the conversions of the original Volkswagen Kombi was undertaken by the Westfalia-werke at the company's

factory in Rheda-Wiedenbrück. Officially contracted by Volkswagen to convert the Transporter into a camper van, Westfalia undertook some 1,000 conversions between the launch of the variant in 1951 and August 1958. Initially, many of these conversions were simply represented by the provision of a box of camping equipment that could be loaded into the Kombi at the weekend and removed come the start of the working week. After 1958, the company introduced a production line, with models being given a special Sonderausführung (SO; Special Model) number. Also, from this date a small square plate was fitted to the vehicle; the so-called M-code plates provide information about the date of manufacture, model and serial number, paint information and much else. If still extant on an original vehicle constructed up to 1976, the plate can be found behind the right-hand front seat; after 1977 the location of the plate was shifted to sit above

THE INSIDE STORY

DEVON CARAVETTE

Turn your week-ends into holidays. Get twice the fun out of life by owning a Caravette.
Luxuriously equipped and finished in hand polished oak, it provides a complete mobile home for a family of four. Deep foam upholstery, tables, cupboards, heater, curtains, a full size double bed plus sleeping accommodation for two children, even a kitchen that includes a cooker, grill, sink unit, food storage and Formica surfaces. Country, mountains, sea-side — make them yours for week-ends — with Volkswagen reliability, independent suspension, synchromesh gears, and an air-cooled engine that can't freeze or boil.
Price? Only £970 complete. No Purchase Tax. Also the DEVONETTE at £819-10-0 on the Volkswagen Kombi.

BUT SEE THE CARAVETTE YOURSELF AT THE MOTOR SHOW — STAND 87

Post this coupon to-day to Volkswagen

Designed and produced by J. P. WHITE LTD. of Sidmouth, Devon
Distributed by
LISBURNE GARAGE
BABBACOMBE ROAD, TORQUAY, DEVON

Please send me without obligation the fully illustrated brochure on the Devon "Caravette"

NAME
ADDRESS
B

VOLKSWAGEN
32-34 St. John's Wood Road, London, N.W.8.   CUNningham 8000
West End Showrooms: 34 Dover Street, London, W.I.   Tel: HYDe Park 1881

■ **TOP:** A typical Westfalia conversion.
■ **ABOVE:** The Devon Caravette.

the air duct on the left-hand side of the vehicle adjacent to the fuse box. Production of the Westfalia continued to boom, particularly after the launch of the replacement Transporter in 1967. Between 1968, when the 30,000th vehicle was converted, and 1971 a total of 70,000 were built, and, in 1971, almost 85% of the production of 22,500 was exported to the USA. Although the relationship had commenced with Volkswagen in the early 1950s, Westfalia gradually developed camper vans based on chassis supplied by other manufacturers; in 2001, Daimler-Chrysler became the sole owner of the business and, two years later, the relationship with Volkswagen ceased with VW taking on the responsibility of producing its own model based around the T5 chassis. Westfalia, however, continue to produce camper vans and other conversions based on other models.

In Britain, one of the leading companies to handle the conversion of the Volkswagen into a camper van was the Sidmouth-based company Devon Conversions Ltd that was established by the cabinet-makers J P White who worked alongside the Torquay-based VW distributors Lisburne Garages. The business was first established in 1956 and by the early 1970s had a market share of some 55% of the UK trade in conversions. The model range included the Moonraker, the Eurovette, the Caravette, the Devonette and the Continental. The original business was sold in 1989 and production transferred to Ferryhill in County Durham. The company is still in business and currently has a product range that includes the Monte Carlo, based upon a Renault chassis, the Aztec, based upon the Fiat Ducator, Citroën Relay or Peugeot Boxer,

■ **RIGHT:** The Danbury conversion.

The latest and best of both worlds

The Danbury conversion for 1972

The latest word:
A comfortable town runabout which handles like a dream. And a beautifully equipped motor caravan that will take you and your family anywhere. Volkswagen reliability, Danbury design ability – the best of both worlds; for travelling, eating, sleeping, relaxing, away from it all.

Come to **STAND 52** at the **MOTOR SHOW** and see my latest Danbury –the most economically priced VW motor caravan conversion on the market today.

George Dawson

Or fill in the coupon for details – and the name of your nearest dealer.

Please send me details of Danbury Motor Caravans

NAME...

ADDRESS...

....

Danbury CONVERSIONS LTD

Danbury Conversions Limited
Danbury, Chelmsford, Essex.

Tel : Danbury 2224/7

the Moonraker, based upon the Volkswagen T5, the Sundowner, also based on the Volkswagen, and the Sapphire, based upon a chassis produced by Mercedes-Benz.

Another noted British manufacturer of conversions is Danbury. Originally based in Essex but now with a factory located just north of Bristol, the company produced its first conversion in 1964 although it is, perhaps, best known for its conversion of the 'Bay' version. Although it offers current models based upon the Volkswagen T5, the Fiat Doblo and the Fiat Scudo, it is still possible to obtain conversions based upon the classic 'Bay' T2 with models offering a variety of packages. These include the Amigo, the Picnicker, the Classic and the SE.

Devon and Danbury were not the only UK companies to produce conversions of the Volkswagen. One of the earliest providers of converted Volkswagens was Peter Pitt. At the time rules governing road vehicles in Britain were complex. If a vehicle was classified as 'commercial' it was restricted to a top speed of 30mph whilst it was also subject to a Purchase Tax (something that passenger cars and motor homes avoided). In addition, vehicles imported incurred an import duty and so much of Pitt's initial work revolved around UK-produced models such as those built by Austin and Commer. In order to qualify as a motor home, the vehicle needed to be equipped with permanent fittings, such as a table and wardrobe. In order to prove that his conversion was a motor home rather than a commercial vehicle, Pitt drove it through Windsor Great Park – which, at the time, had a ban on commercial vehicles – and was prosecuted. Having won the case, Pitt proved that the conversion was indeed not a commercial vehicle and thus escaped from the 30mph ban and the imposition of Purchase

Tax. In 1960, having previously handled Volkswagens occasionally, Pitt, through his company Pitt Moto Caravans, added the VW to his product range. Amongst the facilities that it offered was the

Rising Sunshine Roof; this was a much more flexible device than the elevated roofs on offer from other manufacturers. In 1961, Pitt Moto Caravans merged with Canterbury Sidecars to form Canterbury Pitt

The Volkswagen Transporters

■ **ABOVE:** A VW Transporter ad.

with production shifting to South Ockenden in Essex. Conversions continued through the launch of the Transport T2 in 1967 but were to

cease in February 1969 following Peter Pitt's death.

Other companies included Dormobile, who started to offer a Volkswagen conversion in 1961. Moortown Motors of Leeds was

a Volkswagen distributor that launched a caravan conversion in 1958; later branded as the Autohome, production continued until the mid-1960s. The London-based company European Cars produced a conversion – called the Slumberwagen – between 1958 and 1965. This was based upon the use of the patented Calthorpe elevating roof; Calthorpe also supplied conversions for other models including Bedford, Chevrolet and Commer. It was advertised in the USA with the following sales message: 'Only travel unit in the US that's legal in 50 states as station wagon and never loses its identity as a station wagon. Fast! Easy! The home cruiser's Calthorpe elevating top goes up or down in 2 seconds! When top is raised, it will provide over 6 feet of standing space.'

Based in Ashford, in Middlesex, Richard Holdsworth Conversions first got involved in the provision of conversions in 1967. Five years later the company relocated to a larger site near Reading. Working initially with the 'Bay', the company produced two interior conversion kits – the basic, which lacked a sink but had a pump-tap for a washing-up bowl, and the custom, which included the sink. There were also two options for the roof: a pop top, called the Weathershield, and a single hinged elevating roof that ran the full length of the vehicle. The company continued to produce conversion kits for the T2 through to 1979 when production shifted to work on the T3 (T25). There were again two Holdsworth conversions of this model: the T25 Villa, which also included a chemical toilet and a fridge, and the T25 Vision, which included an area that could be curtained off at the rear of the vehicle for the lavatory. For two years, in 1987/88 and 1988/89, the company won the Motor Caravan of the Year Award but the business was to go into receivership in 1995. Revived as Cockburn Holdsworth, the new enterprise was not to last long.

The final significant company to be involved in the conversion

The Volkswagen Micro Buses

MICRO BUS   There are many ways of making or saving money; operatir VW Micro Bus is one of them, not only one of the best but one of the safest to A bus–above all a Micro Bus–should be more than just a means of low transportation. Whoever travels in it should feel at ease and enjoy the ride. the Volkswagen Micro Bus and the even smarter "De Luxe" provide just amount of comfort which can rightly be expected by a passenger; both give degree of economy which their owners will require.
The double side doors, which open wide and are of generous width, give access to the roomy interior, where passengers can relax in comfortable seats soft, deeply sprung cushions and backrests. The luggage is loaded at the rear the separate luggage compartment, well out of the passengers' way and spac enough to hold 16 average-size suitcases.
Windows of safety glass give full vision all round. One of the most diff problems–air conditioning–has been effectively solved by the adjustable, mounted ventilation system and outward-opening, pivoting and sliding wind thereby doing justice to the demands of even the most exacting passenger. when it gets cold, an efficient heater will spread comfortable warmth.

The pleasing trim of roof and side walls and the interior fittings, which are marked by thoughtful attention to detail, create a truly homely atmosphere that will double your motoring enjoyment.

well balanced front and rear wheel suspension is designed not only to ensure et running of the vehicle but also to convey that feeling of perfect security so ily appreciated by every Volkswagen passenger. A good initial investment, the lkswagen Micro Bus quickly turns out to be a major asset to its owner, doing, e will soon find out, as much as 30 m.p.g. (Imp.)—25 m.p.g. (U.S.), 9.5 lit./100 km.— l carrying as many as eight passengers; experience will soon show him that it dly needs repair even after 60,000 miles or more on the road. No need to worry, ether his bus will safely return from a tour, as he very well knows the ease and ety with which it moves even in the densest traffic. In short, there is nothing like Volkswagen Micro Bus, whatever standards you may apply.

CRO BUS "DE LUXE" There is even more luxury built into the Micro Bus Luxe": windows all round! The skylights fitted with anti-dazzle safety glass. exquisite colour scheme, rich chromium mouldings, and tasteful interior fittings duce that perfect blend which is so characteristic of European styling. tractive and luxurious" — this is the first and lasting impression which people n of the Volkswagen Micro Bus "De Luxe". No doubt, in its class, it is the most dern, most fashionable vehicle for tourist parties.

■ **LEFT:** VW Micro Bus.

■ **ABOVE:** The Devonette.

■ **BELOW:** T25 Holdsworth conversion.

of the Volkswagen into a camper van in the United Kingdom was the Berkhamstead-based Viking Motorhomes. This company entered the market in 1970 and thus worked with the 'Bay' Volkswagen from the start. The new model was designed to increase accommodation from four to six or seven. The company relocated in the early 1970s to Stanbridge, in Bedfordshire, and changed its name to Motorhomes International. The company was perhaps best known for its Spacemaker model – two variants (the Pioneer and the Viking) being available. One of the features of this model was the full-length side-elevating roof; this innovation was, however, to lead to problems with Volkswagen as the German manufacturer claimed that this made the vehicle unstable although these claims were largely dismissed. Motorhomes International continued to produce conversions through until the 1980s with the final conversions featuring the T3.

The Ford Thames 400E was launched in 1957 and was produced at Dagenham until the autumn of 1965. The 15cwt vehicle was ideal for conversion to a motor caravan as its 1703cc engine was powerful enough to handle the additional weight required for the conversion. Amongst companies that produced conversions for the model were Moortown Motors and Peter Pitt, both of whom had also had experience with converting the VW Transporter as well as a number of other companies including Airborne Service Equipment Ltd and Kenex Coachworks Ltd.

Over the years a considerable variety of vehicles have been converted into motor homes or camper vans. One of the smallest must, undoubtedly, be the Mini Van of the 1960s. A firm in Sussex produced a conversion kit – priced

■ **LEFT & BELOW:** Conversions offered from various companies.

from £445 to £601 – that permitted the van to be rebuilt as a motor home. Called the Mini Wildgoose, the vehicle could accommodate a double bed as well as dining area for four people.

Perhaps reflecting the alternative culture that the Volkswagen, in particular, came to reflect, there has been a long tradition of individual customisation of vehicles. At the most basic level this involved the replacement of many of the internal fittings or the repainting of the exterior away from the factory-supplied colours but there's also a desire to stamp one's own individuality upon otherwise anonymous and mass produced vehicles. There is, however, a slight paradox in some of these trends; a fashion for the retro look itself can lead to a degree of uniformity but the reality is that each of these vehicles has been individually altered and so is unique. Amongst the Volkswagen fraternity, for example, there are at least three current strands of serious customisation. Perhaps the most obvious, given the marque's links to the counter-culture of the 1960s and 1970s, is the recreation of vehicles featuring the Hippie

replaced but is enhanced. Beyond the customisation of the exterior of the vehicle and of its interior fixtures and fittings, there is another strand of customisation. This is the group that replaces the standard engine with one with significantly enhanced performance with the intention of using the camper as a racing vehicle. These individuals will often leave the exterior largely untouched, preferring to let the vehicle's prowess on the racetrack do their talking for them.

In terms of customisation, the company Wicked Campers has managed to combine both individuality and commercialism in its range of rental camper vans. Based in Brisbane, in Australia, the company offers travellers the ability to rent cost-effective camper vans in Europe, Australasia, Thailand, Africa and both North and South America. Each of the vans come with a unique hand-painted design; these designs reflect modern music and often incorporate crude slogans. This strategy has made the company highly popular amongst young drivers and back-packers although it hasn't always endeared the business to the authorities!

■ **ABOVE & BELOW:** A conversion of the Mini Van from the 1960s.

■ **LEFT:** The VW Beetle 'California' styling.

motifs of the era. Another strand is the so-called rat-look; here vehicles are aged so that rust is evident – albeit probably carefully nurtured and preserved – and the paintwork is dulled. Everything is done to make the vehicle look down-at-heal. Finally, there is the Cal-look; this is an attempt to recreate the California styling of the 1960s. Although more regularly associated with the Beetle, there are a number of Transporters and camper vans that have undergone this treatment. Here the wheels are changed, the suspension lowered, much of the decorative chrome work dispensed with and the bumpers reduced in size or removed completely. There is a subsidiary version of the Cal-look – the Resto Cal – where the chrome and other decorative work is not only

Afterword

For more than 60 years, the camper van in its various guises has been a hugely popular type of vehicle; for generations it has enabled families to travel the world cheaply and has brought pleasure to countless millions. It has helped to define the modern age in ways that its original proponents could never have dreamed of. The range and quality of vehicles produced over the years and still available today appeal to a wide cross-section of the population. In an age when we have an increasing amount of leisure time, the likelihood is that the camper van – from the most basic Volkswagen conversion through to the massive Recreational Vehicle – is going to be a familiar sight on the world's roads for many more generations to come.

■ **BELOW:** Not a typical conversion, but fun none the less.

Further Information

Books:

Bedford Camper Vans and Motorhomes – The Inside Story; Martin Watts; Crowood Press; 2010

Campervan Crazy: Travels with my Bus – A Tribute to the VW Camper and the People Who Drive Them; David and Cee Eccles; Kyle Cathie Ltd; 2006

Classic Camper Vans – The Inside Story – A Guide to Classic British Campers 1956-1979; Martin Watts; Crowood Press; 2007

Classic Dormobile Camper Vans – A Guide to the Camper Vans of Martin Walter and Dormobile; Martin Watts; Crowood Press; 2009

Europe in a Motor Home: A Mid-life Gap Year Around Southern Europe; H D Jackson; Trafford Publishing; 2006

Home Away from Home: The World of Camper Vans and Motorhomes; Lars Erikson and Kate Trant; Black Dog Publishing; 2005

Motorcaravanning Handbook; John Wickersham; Haynes; 2008

Motor Homes: The Complete Guide; David and Fiona Batten-Hill; Robert Hale Ltd; 2009

The Camper Van Cookbook: Life on Four Wheels, Cooking on Two Rings; Martin Dorey and Sarah Randell; Saltyard Books; 2010

The Motorcaravan Manual: Choosing, Using and Maintaining Your Motorcaravan; John Wickersham; Haynes; 2004

Traveling with the VW Bus & Camper; David and Cee Eccles; Abbeville Press; 2007 (US edition of *Campervan Crazy: Travels with my Bus – A Tribute to the VW Camper and the People Who Drive Them*)

VW Camper – The Inside Story; David Eccles; Crowood Press; 2005

VW Camper and Microbus; Richard A Copping; Shire Library; 2010

VW Camper: Inspirational Interiors; David Eccles; Crowood Press; 2008

VW Camper: Inspirational Interiors; David Eccles; Crowood Press; 2011

Volkswagen Camper – 40 Years of Freedom: An A-Z of Popular Camper Conversions; Richard Copping; Veloce; 2007

VW Transporter and Microbus Specification Guide; David Eccles; Crowood Press; 2004

VW Transporter: The Legendary Type 2 1950-1982; Laurence Meredith; Crowood Press; 2005

Magazines:

MMM: Motorcaravan Motorhome Monthly; Warners Group; monthly

Practical Motorhome; Haymarket; monthly

Volkswagen Camper & Commercial; Jazz Publishing; bi-monthly

Volksworld Camper & Bus; IPC Media; monthly

Websites:

www.campervanlife.com

www.classcampers.com

www.dormobile.org.uk

www.camperinterior.co.uk

www.volkszone.com

www.westfaliat3.info

www.camperinterior.webfotos.co.uk

www.volksculture.com